MW00909795

Activities
for the

Cape Cod

Beachcomber

Gilbert Newton

Dedication

*This book is dedicated
to all my students,
young and young at heart,
for their curiosity and
sense of discovery.*

Thank you to Nancy Shoemaker for her photographs –
and her professional advice and guidance in the design
and creation of all my books.

Published by Gilbert Newton
gdnewton@comcast.net

Copyright 2020 by Gilbert Newton
All rights reserved.
Published in the United States 2020.

ISBN 978-1-7328701-1-6

This book produced by Nancy Viall Shoemaker, West Barnstable Press
www.westbarnstablepress.com

Table of Contents

E. Farrin

Introduction

Knowledge and awareness of the local natural environment is essential for the stewardship and protection of our important ecosystems. The threats to their stability is global, but local attention and understanding will help meet the challenges facing all of us. To that end I have always believed in the power of an educated population. We can successfully address these mounting environmental problems by learning and studying through direct contact with nature.

I think back to my childhood on Cape Cod when the outdoors held a magical quality which endlessly stimulated my curiosity. I was fascinated by the ocean, the weather, and the plants and animals that I encountered during my explorations. I dug for worms, captured fireflies, and inspected bird nests. I walked continuously through the pine woods, around kettle hole ponds, into open meadows and fields, and often to the dynamic seashore.

Teaching others to learn, care, and cherish the natural environment became my avocation, passion, and career. Nothing can substitute for direct observation and experience in nature when it comes to understanding how living things interact with the physical environment and with each other.

And one of the most interesting places to learn and study is the coastal marine environment. The diversity of marine habitats contains assemblages of plants and animals that can be easily examined with careful observations and simple equipment. The various activities in this book are all "hands-on" and can be conducted throughout the year, at many locations and during different physical conditions.

The most important rule is to explore with an open mind. Take your time. Become familiar with your surroundings. Hone your observation skills. And you will find as you embark on your beachcombing journey a fascinating and exciting world just waiting to be explored.

Gil Newton

A list of materials needed as you get ready to explore:

1. A bucket and a tray for collecting
2. A hand lens (5x or 10x)
3. A ruler or measuring tape
4. Field guides (See page 61)
5. A notebook and pencil
6. A dip net for collecting
7. Water shoes or boots
8. Sunscreen lotion and insect/tick repellent
9. Protective clothing for variations in weather

Gil Newton

While beachcombing can be done at any time of the year, certain precautions and planning should always be considered.

1. Children should be accompanied by an adult.
2. Observe all property rights. Obey "No Trespassing" signs.
3. If collecting and observing any live animals, return them to the same location.
4. Be careful when walking on rocks or jetties. They can be very slippery.
5. Strong surf and currents should be avoided.
6. Wear water shoes or boots to avoid cuts by broken glass or sharp shells and rocks.
7. Be mindful of areas with a large tidal range. Don't get stranded by a fast-moving high tide!
8. Be aware of any local laws that restrict access or activities such as collecting. Digging for shellfish may require a permit even if you are not keeping the shellfish.
9. Adults should be familiar with any parking regulations. Some places have seasonal parking fees or require passes.
10. Don't trample any coastal plants that are important for erosion control and for wildlife habitat.

A Changing Beach

Beaches are dynamic systems that are formed by the accumulation of sand. They are constantly being moved. The size and composition of beach materials varies and is influenced by storms, wind, waves, currents, and human-made construction such as jetties, groins, and sea walls. A jetty is a constructed rock formation located at the mouth of an inlet and is often composed of large boulders.

1. Locate a beach system that has human influence such as a jetty.

2. Describe the beach sediments. Are they sandy, rocky, or muddy? Does the beach have sections where all three sediment types can be seen?

3. Jetties were originally designed to control erosion, but there is ample evidence to show that they actually increase erosion by focusing wave energy on a narrower section of the beach.

4. Examine the effects of the jetty present. Do you see any signs of erosion?

5. Is there a buildup of sand, seaweed, or shells on one side of the jetty?

6. Have the finer grain sands been removed, leaving behind larger stones and rocks? If so, this would then be designated a cobble beach.

7. Are there any animals, such as crabs, living under these rocks?

8. Have any algae or animals colonized the rock jetty?

9. Look for the presence of rockweed and barnacles on the jetty. How are they distributed? Do they co-exist or are they attached in separate sections?

10. The slope of the beach may also be affected by the presence of jetties and storm activity. Sometimes an elevated ridge of sand known as a berm can form. Do you see any signs of a berm? Is this more conspicuous in summer or winter?

11. Are there any signs of animal life along the shore?

12. Sometimes small pools of water get trapped at high tide in a jetty. Look for these and the presence of sponges, sea anemones, and sea stars.

NOTES: _____

_____

_____

_____

_____

_____

_____

_____

A Coastal Ecological Eye

The coastal environment is characterized by change. It is constantly re-formed and re-structured by waves, wind, and weather. And in this dynamic system one can find and observe a wide variety of marine life with specialized adaptations. Paying close attention will help you develop an "ecological eye."

1. Visit a nearby coastal site such as a beach system or estuary.

2. Bring a field notebook with you to record your observations — and a ruler for measurements.

3. Describe the habitat(s) you observe and make a sketch of the area. Be as specific as possible.

4. What plants and animals do you see? Even if only a part of an animal is present can you identify it? Make a sketch and record its size, color, shape, and condition.

NVS

5. Record information about the tides, weather, and sediment type.

6. Are there differences in the kinds of plants and animals you see at different sections of the area? Describe these.

7. What is the most common plant? How is it adapted to this habitat?

8. What is the most common animal? How is it adapted to this habitat?

9. What human influences do you observe?

10. Based on your observations, do you think this is a sustainable resource or is it threatened by human activity?

NOTES: _____

_____

_____

_____

_____

_____

_____

_____

_____

_____

_____

_____

_____

_____

_____

_____

Keeping Records

One of the most valuable ways of learning about the environment is to keep a journal or log of observations. This is particularly beneficial over a long period of time in which changes in the habitat can be recorded as well as notations on specific plants and animals. A notebook could be simply a blank sheet of paper or a more detailed data sheet in which specific questions are answered.

NVS

1. Identify an undisturbed area that can be observed over time.

2. Before you use a field guide to identify an unknown plant or animal, make your own set of observations. This is more effective than thumbing through a book looking at pictures.

3. If it's a plant, try to observe and record information about it when it first appears. Then follow its growth throughout the season.

4. When observing animals, use a hand lens to look for specific features such as the shape of a claw, the size of a shell, or the presence of other attached species.

5. Are there variations within the population of the same species?

6. Are there signs of feeding? For example, do some shells exhibit small holes suggesting the work of a predator?

7. Use your observations and a field guide to identify each species and keep an ongoing list.

8. Does the assemblage of species change with different weather conditions or tides?

NOTES: _____

_____

_____

_____

_____

_____

_____

_____

_____

_____

_____

_____

_____

_____

_____

_____

Adopt a Beach

Have you ever been to your favorite beach and wondered what critters spend their lives there? Is this area popular with others, so much so that they leave trash behind after visiting? How can you help protect and preserve this natural resource that is meaningful to you and others?

One way is to learn as much as you can about a particular beach, or section of a beach, and be a self-appointed guardian. You can also help educate others with your knowledge and commitment. And you can provide a continuous ecological patrol of the area.

1. Select a site. It can be of any size, but make it an area that you can easily and frequently visit to patrol and monitor.

2. Do a quick survey of any living plants or animals in the area and make a list of all the species that you observe.

3. Describe any difference you see during:
   a. high and low tides
   b. time of day
   c. seasons
   d. weather conditions

NVS

4. What are the most common plant and animal species? Do you see these represented most of the time?

5. Keep a field notebook of any changes that you observe. Try to visit the site periodically for about one year.

6. Are there seasonal differences in the distribution of species?

7. Are there any species that wash up after a storm?

8. Look carefully with a hand lens at any seaweed that washes up. Are there tiny plants or animals that are attached? Can you identify them?

9. Be careful as you examine the seaweed. Wear protective gloves during this part of the activity. The seaweed can trap floating debris.

10. Review your data log after each season and after one year. What changes do you see? Are the same plants and animals present after one year? Were there some species that appeared only seasonally?

NOTES: _____

_____

_____

_____

_____

_____

_____

_____

_____

_____

Seaweeds are not Plants

Seaweeds (macroalgae) use chlorophyll and can photosynthesize like true plants, but they lack the conducting structures known as vascular tissue (xylem and phloem). Seaweeds are placed in the kingdom Protista and do not have true leaves, stems, roots, flowers, fruits, or seeds. Many seaweed structures resemble these plant parts but have different names.

1. Collect a variety of seaweeds and place in a tray. Try to collect the different colors: green, brown, and red. Look for seaweeds with different shapes as well.

2. Identify the phyla or division for each seaweed:
   Green - Chlorophyta
   Brown - Phaeophyta
   Red - Rhodophyta

3. Most seaweeds are attached to a strong object or the substrate by a root-like structure called a holdfast. Locate the holdfast on each seaweed.

4. Describe each holdfast. How are they similar? How are they different?

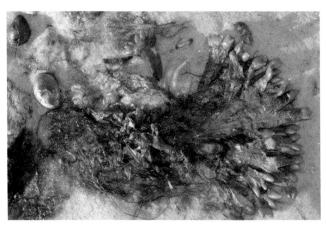

NVS

5. Locate the stem-like structure called a stipe on each alga. Do they have a line going down the middle? That's called a midrib. Do any of the seaweeds have branches?

6. The leaf-like part of the seaweed is the blade or frond. How do they differ?

7. Examine the frond closely with a hand lens. Are there any animals attached such as bryozoans or hydroids? You might see signs of small polyps.

8. Are there any smaller seaweeds attached? These are called epiphytes.

9. Several brown algae species such as the rockweeds and kelps may contain air or gas bladders (pneumatocysts) for flotation. Locate the air bladders.

10. Measure the size of the air bladders. Are they all the same size?

11. Return to the beach. Where along the intertidal zone (area between high and low tide) do you find most of the green algae?

12. Describe the locations of the brown and red algae species.

NOTES: _____

_____

_____

_____

_____

_____

_____

_____

_____

Life in the Wrackline

Ascophyllum nodosum is commonly called knotted wrack. The fronds can grow up to three feet long and are characterized by several large and single air bladders, but there is no distinct midrib like in *Fucus*, another common rockweed. *Ascophyllum* is an important seaweed for other  forms of marine life that find shelter under its fronds. This provides them with protection from predators and keeps them moist at low tide on warm days. For this activity, bring the following to the beach: a small bucket, a hand lens or magnifying glass, a few small cups, and a pair of forceps or tweezers.

1. Gather a small pile of knotted wrack that has recently washed up on the beach.

2. Place it in a bucket of seawater and let it sit for about an hour. Some small animals may be seen swimming in the water.

3. Separate any larger animals from the seaweed, such as sponges, seashells, or parts of crabs, and place them in the cups.

4. Carefully remove a small branch of the rockweed and use a hand lens to examine it.

5. Are there any small plants or animals attached to the branch?

6. An interesting group of animals are the moss animals, so named because they are often confused with seaweeds, yet they belong to the animal group, the bryozoans.

7. Again using the hand lens look for a brown, bushy colony of a moss animal called *Bugula neritina* which may be attached to the seaweed. Do you see any polyps?

8. Are there any marine sponges found in the wrack line? It's possible to find the colorful redbeard sponge (*Microciona prolifera*) and the lightly colored deadman's fingers (*Haliclona occulata*).

9. Use the hand lens to examine any small attached seaweeds (epiphytes). One associated with *Ascophyllum* is the tiny red seaweed *Polysiphonia linosa*. With the hand lens you can observe small red bands along the branches.

10. Record and draw any other species seen.

11. Return all living samples with the seaweed to the marine environment where they were collected.

NOTES: _____

_____

_____

_____

_____

_____

_____

_____

_____

_____

Examining Rockweed

The common rockweed (*Fucus vesiculosus*) grows in the muddy banks of salt marshes as well as on jetties, pilings, and other hard surfaces. The brown forked branches have pairs of small air bladders along the midrib of the frond which help the alga float in the water. The alga is attached to the substrate by a root-like holdfast. The swollen tips are called receptacles and contain the reproductive cells.

1. Locate a population of rockweed at low tide and describe its habitat.

2. Is the alga growing in extensive clumps or is it distributed randomly in this area?

3. Identify the following structures:
    a. frond
    b. air bladders
    c. holdfast
    d. receptacle
    e. midrib

4. How are the air bladders arranged along the midrib?

5. Do you see small bumps on the receptacles? If so, these are the conceptacles and contain the male and female reproductive cells.

6. Carefully lift a clump of rockweed without removing it from the substrate.

7. Do you see any of the following animals: ribbed mussels, barnacles, sand hoppers, or attached bryozoans?

8. Why are these animals living underneath the rockweed?

9. Use a hand lens and look carefully at the rockweed branches.

10. Do you see a small curly white case attached to the fronds? This is the tube worm *Spirorbus*.

11. Are there any other animals attached such as barnacles?

12. Are there any smaller seaweeds attached such as different species of red algae?

13. Even though rockweed is brown, it is a producer and makes its own food through the process of photosynthesis. How do the air bladders help this process?

14. Are there other seaweeds in this habitat?

15. Why are different kinds of rockweeds, particularly the knotted wrack (*Ascophyllum nodosum*), used as packing material for clams and lobsters?

NOTES: _____

_____

_____

_____

_____

_____

_____

_____

The Seaweed Herbarium

There is an easy and fun way to preserve seaweeds for study and use. Creating a seaweed herbarium allows the beachcomber to collect various species at different seasons and to press them so that they last for several years.

1. Acquire the following materials:
   a. a tray at least one inch deep
   b. cheese cloth or wax paper
   c. paper made of a thick stock
   d. newspapers
   e. scissors
   f. bucket to carry seaweeds
   g. several heavy books

2. Collect whole specimens of seaweeds that have not been bleached or decomposed.

3. Transport the seaweed back home in a bucket of salt water.

4. Put some of the seawater in the tray and float the seaweed on top.

5. Cut a section of thick paper and place it in the water under the seaweed.

6. Slowly raise the paper and gently arrange the seaweed the way you want it pressed. A small medicine dropper can help you arrange any fine filaments.

7. Carefully remove the paper and drain the excess water off the sides.

8. Cut a section of cheese cloth or wax paper and cover the seaweed. The cheese cloth works better as the seaweed is less likely to stick to it.

9. Gently tap on this covering.

10. Place the specimen between two sheets of newspaper and close.

11. Place some heavy books on the newspaper.

12. Change the newspaper each day for two days. This helps absorb any moisture.

13. After a couple of days carefully peel the cheese cloth off the specimen. The seaweed should stick to the paper.

14. You can combine different species in the same paper.

15. Please note that this process works best for fine, filamentous algae, but is difficult for any thick or large seaweeds.

NOTES: _____

_____

_____

_____

_____

_____

_____

_____

_____

_____

Coral Weed

Coral weed (*Corallina officinalis*) is a common calcifying red alga often found attached to periwinkle snails. It has the ability to remove calcium carbonate (limestone) out of the water column and deposit it around its soft tissues. Coral weed can often be collected in and around tide pools near jetties. You will need a hand lens for this activity.

1. Describe the habitat where you collected *Corallina*.

2. To what object is it attached, or was it floating in the water?

3. Is the specimen alive or dead? It is dark purple if alive and bleached white if dead.

4. Examine the branches closely with a hand lens.

5. What is the largest branch?

6. How many joints are along the branch?

7. Do these connecting points contain calcium carbonate or are they free to move?

8. How would you describe this unusual seaweed?

9. Do you see other seaweeds that can calcify or is this the only one?

10. How common was your find? Were there several samples available or was it scarce?

11. Based on your observations, what local environmental conditions are suitable for the growth of *Corallina*?

12. How do you think this ability to calcify helps the seaweed adapt to its environment?

NOTES: _____

_____

_____

_____

_____

_____

_____

_____

_____

_____

_____

_____

_____

_____

Aging a Quahog

Quahogs (*Mercenaria mercenaria*) are economically important shellfish that are adapted to the changing salinity in a  salt marsh. Their thick shells also have a purple lining on the inside, and can grow up to four inches long. Quahogs can live up to two decades. The approximate age can be determined by examining the distinct growth rings on the outside of the shell.

1. Collect a series of quahog shells of different sizes. Collect at least five shells.

2. Measure the length of each shell and determine the specific name for the quahog:

   a. littlenecks - up to one and a half inches.
   b. cherrystones - between one and a half and two and a half inches
   c. chowder - three inches or more

3. Which one was the most common that you found?

4. Were they all located in the same area or at different sections of the beach or marsh?

5. As the clam grows each year so does its shell. A new ring or thick band surrounded by finer bands shows on the shell each year. Each thick band is one year's growth. By counting them you can estimate its age.

6. Arrange the quahog shells from smallest to largest.

7. Count the thick bands on each shell. You may need to run your thumb across the bands to determine the thickest. Some of the bands will exist in bunches producing a thick band.

8. Estimate the age of each shell. How old is the youngest? The oldest?

9. What is the average age for your collection?

10. What would happen if the shell of the quahog did not get bigger each year?

11. What environmental conditions will affect the growth of the quahog?

12. What advantages does an animal with a shell have?

NOTES: _____

_____

_____

_____

_____

_____

_____

_____

_____

Mussel Beach

Embedded in the banks of a salt marsh are large clumps of ribbed mussels (*Modiolus demissus*). These animals are attached to the peat and to each other by strong byssal threads. Ribbed mussels are cylindrical,  and the shells have ridges or ribs along their length.

1. Locate a group of ribbed mussels along the banks of a salt marsh.

2. How would you describe their distribution: uniform, clumped, or random?

3. Can you find the byssal threads attached to them? If so, how strong are they?

4. Are there any other animals attached to their shells?

5. Are the mussels visible or camouflaged in the marsh? What is the advantage of this condition?

6. Count the number of bands along the outside of the shell. Approximately how old is that mussel?

7. The width in the bands varies from year to year. What conditions might cause the bands to be larger?

8. What advantage does an animal with a shell have?

9. Are there any predators present that might consume the mussels?

10. What size is the largest ribbed mussel in the area?

11. Where along the marsh is it located?

NOTES: _____

_____

_____

_____

_____

_____

_____

_____

_____

_____

_____

_____

_____

Claws not Jaws

Some of the most common finds at a beach are the remains of coastal crabs. The "shell" of the crab is called a carapace. This exoskeleton is composed of a material called chitin. There are three major parts to a crab: the head, thorax, and abdomen. Because these animals are often a favorite food for shorebirds, you may find just parts of a crab.

1. Explore the shoreline for any parts of a crab. Be sure to look in the wrackline. Try to find samples of different crab legs and shells.

2. Describe the differences between the legs. Three common crabs can be distinguished by color:
   a. Blue crabs (*Callinectes sapidus*) - blue
   b. Green crabs (*Carcinus maenus*) - green
   c. Spider crabs (*Libinia emarginata*) - brown

3. Measure the length of each leg and compare.

4. Which leg is the longest? The thickest?

5. If you have any samples of hind legs, are they paddle shaped? Blue crabs and lady crabs (*Ovalipes ocellatus*) have this characteristic.

6. Examine the "shell" or carapace of any crab.

7. Describe each shape and measure the length.

8. How many teeth or spines along each edge? A blue crab has nine teeth along each margin. A green crab has five teeth along the margin.

9. Describe the habitat of each crab found. If in a marsh you might locate a fiddler crab (*Uca pugnax*). The male crab has a large claw which is not seen in the female.

10. Based on your description of a claw, can you predict the animal's food source?

11. Look for living examples of the species you found. Where are they located?

12. Do any of the crab shells have "hitchhikers", that is other animals attached to them?

NOTES: _____

_____

_____

_____

_____

_____

_____

_____

_____

_____

The Sedentary Crustacean

The barnacle (*Semibalanus balanoides*) is the only crustacean that stays in place for its entire adult life. A single barnacle will spend its adult life in an upside position, its head cemented to a rock while moving its feathery legs to capture small food particles. At high tide the legs are beating in the water, trapping phytoplankton,

while at low tide they close, protecting the animal within from desiccation. Barnacles tend to settle and grow in areas that are already inhabited by other barnacle colonies.

1. Locate an area where there is an extensive barnacle colony. Describe the habitat.

2. Is the colony uniformly distributed or does it exist in patches?

3. Do the barnacles in the colony differ in size? If so, where are the largest ones located?

4. Measure the length of the opening (operculum) of the largest and smallest barnacle and compare.

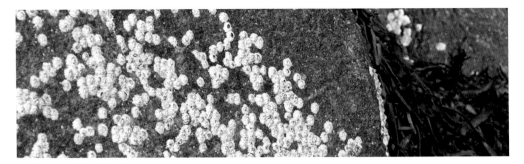

5. Which of these will be more efficient at feeding?

6. Describe the plates that make up the external structure.

7. How large is the barnacle colony? Measure its length.

8. Count the number of barnacles in a one-meter squared area close to the shore and in another one-meter square area beneath the low water mark. Compare.

9. Are there other plant or animal species present? Name them.

10. Are there barnacles co-existing with rockweed?

11. Do these barnacles live above, below, or underneath the rockweed?

12. Can you find barnacle populations living in different habitats?

NOTES: _____

_____

_____

_____

_____

_____

_____

_____

_____

_____

_____

_____

Anybody Home?

There are several common gastropods or snails found on beaches. Knobbed whelks (*Busycon carica*) and channeled whelks (*Busycon canaliculatum*) are two of the largest. The major physical difference is that the knobbed whelk has bumps or knobs on the outer shell. These are carnivorous animals and feed on various bivalves by using their shells to break open the clams for feeding. They also feed by using a radula, a small

toothed structure. Occasionally you can find their long brown egg cases in which each capsule contains several young whelks.

1. Locate a whelk egg case with several capsules attached.

2. Examine a capsule. Can you see any tiny objects inside?

3. What is the shape of the capsule?

4. Measure its width.

5. How many capsules are there attached to each other?

6. Examine the edges of each capsule. If there are two conspicuous edges on each disk-shaped capsule, it's a knobbed whelk. If only one sharp edge, it's a channeled whelk. Which do you have?

7. Using a small pair of scissors, cut open one of the capsules.

8. How many young whelks are present?

9. Cut open several capsules, count the contents of each, and calculate an average.

10. If there are no young whelks present can you observe an opening to the capsule?

11. Measure the total length of the egg case.

12. Was the egg case floating in the water or entangled in seaweed?

13. What time of year did you find the egg case?

14. Are there any whelk shells at the location?

NOTES: _____

_____

_____

_____

_____

_____

_____

_____

_____

_____

_____

The Primitive Horseshoe Crab

Nearly 400 million years after it evolved, the horseshoe crab (*Limulus polyphemus*) is a common animal on the northeast coast. Horseshoe crabs are not true crabs, but are more closely related to spiders and scorpions. They have five pairs of legs for crawling, and a set of book gills for breathing and swimming. The animal grows by molting from the head first. The molt is much lighter than the original animals, and the opening is easily seen.

1. Locate a horseshoe crab shell and examine its structure.

2. Do you have a molt or a whole animal?

3. How many pairs of walking legs are there?

4. Are there any signs of attached animals on the horseshoe crab?

5. If so, can you identify them?

6. Do these "hitchhikers" have an advantage by attaching themselves?

7. Does the horseshoe crab benefit from these animals or is it not affected at all?

8. Identify and draw the following structures:
   a) carapace
   b) compound eyes
   c) book gills
   d) telson (tail)

9. If you find parts of a horseshoe crab, can you identify the parts?

10. What do you think happened to the animal?

11. What is the correct way of holding a live horseshoe crab?

12. Is the specimen a male or female? Males have a modified claw that has been compared to a boxing glove, whereas the female's appendages are shaped as pincers.

NOTES: _____

_____

_____

_____

_____

_____

_____

_____

_____

_____

_____

At a Snail's Pace

The common periwinkle snail (*Littorina littorea*) is found mainly along a rocky substrate on jetties, groins, and sea walls. This tiny snail grows a little over an inch long. Its shell is dark and spiral. It contains a foot for movement, a protective operculum over the shell opening, and a radula for scraping microscopic algae and bacteria off the seaweeds and rocks.

1. Locate a habitat that contains a large population of periwinkles.

2. How are they grouped (random, uniform, or clumped)?

3. Does this grouping vary with temperature?

4. Place one of the snails on a paper plate and observe its movements.

5. Observe and describe the following:
   a) foot
   b) sensory tentacles
   c) shape of shell

6. Take another look at its habitat. Is there an abundant seaweed population, or does the area look like it's been grazed?

7. Collect several snail shells. Measure sizes of the openings.

8. Does this vary with the overall size of the animal or is it consistently the same?

9. Temporarily set up a marked area. You can use stakes. However, I recommend that you use a natural landmark such as a large boulder to identify the site when you return and don't leave any stakes or materials behind.

10. Count all the periwinkles in the site.

11. Using a bright red nail polish, mark each one with a clear visible dot on the outside of the shell. This will not harm the animal.

12. Record the number of marked periwinkles in a notebook.

13. In the next day or two, visit the same site and count the number of marked periwinkles as well as the number of unmarked animals. Record the total number (marked plus unmarked).

14. Use the following units:
    P = total population of periwinkles at the site
    M = total number of marked periwinkles
    p = total number of periwinkles at second visit
    m = total number of marked individuals recaptured at second visit

15. Calculate the estimated population of periwinkle snails using this formula: P= Mxp/m (x=multiply).
    This formula is known as the Lincoln Index.

16. Record the tide and weather conditions for each day, particularly the temperature.

17. Were the perwinkles still in the same area, or did they move to another spot?

NOTES: _____

_____

_____

_____

_____

_____

Spiny Skin Animal

Sea stars or starfish (*Asterias vulgaris*) are found in tide pools or protected areas in the crevices of rock jetties. Sea stars love to feed on bivalve mollusks, particularly mussels. Their arms or rays attach to the mussel, pry it open, and slide their stomach inside the mussel to digest it. Sea stars are echinoderms, marine animals with

an endoskeleton and small tube feet on the ventral side that are used for motion. Sea stars also have an elaborate series of internal canals for the movement of water called a water vascular system.

1. Collect a live sea star and place it in a tray. Remember to return the animal to the same location when finished with the activity.

2. Identify the central disk and the rays or arms.

3. How many arms are there?

4. Measure the length of each arm.

5. Are they all the same length? If there is one that is very short or missing, explain why.

6. Use the hand lens and look at the tip of an arm. You should see a red eyespot. What is its function?

7. Examine the upper or dorsal side. Do you see a small round disk close to the center? This is called a madreporite or sieve plate which is the entrance to the water vascular system. What is its color?

8. Examine the lower or ventral side. Locate the tube feet and describe them. What is their function?

9. Was the animal feeding when you collected it? What was its food source?

10. Were there several sea stars present or only one?

11. Sea stars are characterized by radial symmetry. What does that mean? (*Hint:* think of spokes on a bicycle wheel).

12. Describe the sea star habitat.

13. What other animals were present in this habitat?

14. Name other examples of echinoderms.

NOTES: _____

_____

_____

_____

_____

_____

_____

_____

_____

_____

_____

_____

Dust on the Dunes

Dusty miller (*Artemisia stelleriana*) is a pale green perennial plant that grows primarily on dunes and sandy soil. It is also a favorite garden plant in sandy habitats. The leaves are covered with small white hairs and are round at the tips. They grow close to the ground and function effectively in preventing erosion from wind and storms. Flowers are small and yellow on a stalk and are wind-pollinated. The plants are grown in gardens primarily for their foliage. When examining any plants on a sand dune caution should be exercised to avoid trampling the plants. Check for tiny deer ticks, a dune being one of their primary habitats. Dusty miller can often be found growing along the edges of dunes, so check there first for the plants.

1. Rub your fingers along one of the leaves. How would you describe its texture?

2. Do you detect numerous hairs? What do you think is their function?

3. Some observers compare the surface of a sand dune to that of a desert. How are these two environments similar?

4. How does a plant like dusty miller survive in the harsh environment?

5. Are there any flowers present? If so, how would you describe them?

6. How would you describe the distribution of dusty miller on the dune?

7. Are there any other plant species growing nearby?

8. If so, how are they similar? How are they different?

9. Why is it an advantage for dusty miller to grow close to the ground?

NOTES: _____

_____

_____

_____

_____

_____

_____

_____

_____

_____

Moss Production

Mosses are an important group of small plants that can grow along the edges of coastal banks and woodlands near the shore. These tiny plants lack specialized cells that carry food and water, so they don't have any true leaves, stems, roots, flowers, fruits, and seeds. Instead, they produce leaf-like structures, and long stalks with a cap that releases spores for reproduction. Mosses have chlorophyll so they make their own food through the process of photosynthesis. They provide food and shelter for small animals. They also help prevent erosion while contributing to soil formation.

1. Look for mosses along the upper edge of a woodland or coastal bank where it meets the beach or shore. Some coastal banks just above a salt marsh may also contain mosses.

2. What do you notice about the growth habit of the plant? Is it in single rows or large mats and clumps?

3. Examine a single moss plant closely with a hand lens.

GDN

4. Is it producing stalks with caps?

5. Carefully shake one of the caps on a plain index card. Do
    you see any spores?

6. Are mosses growing along the base of any trees on the
    coastal bank?

7. Do you see any animals in the moss population?

8. Do these mosses that grow close to the coastline differ
    from those that grow in the middle of a woodland or
    near a freshwater system?

9. Are there any lichens growing with the mosses? If so,
    describe them.

10. Based on your observations, how are mosses ecologically
    important in this environment?

NOTES: _____

_____

_____

_____

_____

_____

_____

_____

_____

_____

_____

_____

_____

Plants in Winter

Winter is a very harsh time of year for plants in the northeast, particularly in habitats such as sand dunes. While most parts of plants die back in winter, several other parts have adapted to the heavy snows and cold winds. One of the most important adaptations is the prevention of water loss to

GDN

protect the living tissues inside. Many of the dune plant species retain the above-ground part to protect the sand from eroding away in harsh weather.

1. Examine the characteristics of a plant on a dune in winter.

2. Are there any leaves still on the plant?

3. If so, is this plant an evergreen or are the leaves brown and still clinging to the branches?

NVS

4. Do the leaves fold downward? If that is the case, how does that help the plant survive in the winter?

5. If there are no leaves on the plant, look for the place where they were once attached. These are known as leaf scars.

6. Can you tell from the leaf scars if the leaves were alternate, opposite, or whorled?

7. Are there any dried fruits, pods, or seeds? Look for rose hips, for example. If present, describe their shape.

8. If all the seeds are gone, what do you think happened to them?

9. Some plants in late winter begin to show buds. Can you locate any of these?

10. Based on your observations, can you determine if it was insect pollinated or wind pollinated? What would you look for?

NOTES: _____

_____

_____

_____

_____

_____

_____

_____

_____

_____

_____

_____

_____

_____

Plant Invaders

There are several species of invasive plants that can result in the loss of bio-diversity in a coastal ecosystem. These plant invaders all have certain features in common. They are well adapted to a wide range of environmental conditions, often flourishing in poor soils and periods of drought. They may have structural features which increase their adaptation success, such as a long taproot or a very high seed production. They can quickly out compete rival plants for space, water, and nutrients.

One of the most notorious plant invaders on the east coast of the U.S. is the common reed (*Phragmites australis*). This tall, common grass grows around freshwater, brackish water, and even salt marsh systems. It is extremely invasive and can grow in astounding densities.

1. Locate a population of *Phragmites* near a coastal wetland.

2. Describe the habitat in which it is found.

3. Using four meter sticks or a tape measure, square off an area surrounding the plants.

4. Count all the individual plants within the one meter square unit. This is the density measured by the number of plants per meter squared.

5. Do the same for the outer edge of the plant population's growth as well as the thickest area.

6. Compare your results.

7. Does it appear that the plants are spreading? For example, do you see young shoots appearing along the edges of the area?

8. Are there any other plants growing there? If so, do you think they have enough space and sunlight to survive?

9. Are there flowers or seeds present on the *Phragmites*?

10. Are these seeds distributed by the wind or animals?

11. If it is allowed in the area, dig up one of the plants and describe its root system. Is it extensive, shallow, or branching?

12. Are there any other features of the plant that would suggest it is very competitive?

13. Are there any animals such as insects living in the *Phragmites*?

14. Are there any birds present?

NOTES: _____

_____

_____

_____

_____

_____

_____

_____

The Invasive Greenbrier

Greenbrier (*Smilax rotundifolia*) is a common invasive plant that can grow profusely around the edges of salt marshes, woodlands and open fields. Greenbrier can form huge thick stands that are nearly impossible to walk through. These thickets tend to grow inward, adding another layer of shrubbery that blocks the growth of smaller herbaceous plants.

1. Locate a greenbrier shrub and take a close look.

2. Are the leaves simple (single whole blade) or compound (blade divided into a number of leaflets)?

3. Are there thorns along the stem?

4. Are there bluish fruits (berries) present?

5. Open a few of them. How many seeds in each berry?

6. Do you observe any birds consuming the berries?

7. How would you describe the shape of the leaf?

8. Describe how the leaves are arranged:
   a) alternate - one leaf attached to the stem.
   b) opposite - two leaves at the same point of attachment
   c) whorled - three or more leaves attached at same point.

9. Examine the tendrils (thin coiling structures) with a hand lens. What do they cling to?

10. Do the tendrils grow clockwise or counterclockwise?

11. Do the tendrils have disks at their base?

12. Can you trace a tendril to the parent plant?

NOTES: _____

_____

_____

_____

_____

_____

_____

_____

_____

_____

_____

_____

_____

_____

Seaside Roses

Salt spray rose (*Rosa rugosa*) is a common shrub growing in sandy soil along the coastline. Introduced from eastern Asia, this shrub grows from three to seven feet high. Like many rose species, the stems are covered with sharp thorns. The white, pink, or red flowers may be three to four inches in length and bloom for most of the summer into early fall. The fruits are called rose hips and appear late in the growing season. Rose hips are used in the making of jams and jellies.

This is a hardy shrub and is quite tolerant of salt spray, dry conditions, and variations in temperature.

1. Locate a salt spray rose plant on a sandy dune.

2. Measure the air and soil temperatures and compare them.

3. Are the leaves simple or compound?

4. Measure the length of several thorns and average them. What is the largest thorn measured?

5. Do all the roses on the dune have the same flower color or do they differ?

6. If rose hips are present, how large are they?

7. Measure several rose hips and calculate the average. Compare them with the other roses on the dune.

8. Does the plant produce flowers and fruits at the same time?

9. Are there any insects present? Are any of them pollinating the rose?

10. Are there any signs of insect damage on the leaves or fruits?

11. Salt spray rose is sometimes considered an invasive plant. Are there any other plant species nearby on the dune?

12. Do the rose flowers have any scent?

13. Describe these shrubs in winter conditions.

14. Where on the dune do most of the roses grow?

NOTES: _____

_____

_____

_____

_____

_____

_____

_____

_____

_____

_____

_____

_____

_____

Common Gold

Seaside goldenrod (*Solidago sempervirens*) is a common wildflower growing on coastal sand dunes and banks. It is a member of the family Asteraceae which is also called the sunflower family and used to be named the Compositae. That is because the "flower" in this group really consists of a composite of two different kinds of flowers. Inside the inflorescence are tiny disk flowers. These are surrounded by petal-like ray flowers. The fruit is called an achene and contains a single seed which is distributed by the wind.

1. Locate a population of flowering seaside goldenrod on a dune.

2. How are the plants distributed?

3. Do they co-exist with other plant species or are they in separate colonies?

4. Measure the height of several plants and calculate the average.

5. Examine goldenrod's leaves. How would you describe their texture?

6. What is the average length of the leaves?

7. Are the leaves mainly basal or are they uniform along the stem?

8. Is the leaf arrangement opposite or alternate?

9. Examine one of the floral inflorescences with a hand lens.

10. Locate the ray flowers and the disk flowers.

11. On average how many ray flowers are there?

12. Are there any pollinators on the plants? What species do you see?

13. Do you think this plant is effective in preventing erosion on the dune? Why or why not?

14. Describe the adaptations goldenrod has for growing on a sand dune.

CAUTION:

1. *Sand dune plant communities are fragile and extra effort should be made to avoid trampling any vegetation.*

2. *Do not remove any plants from the dune as they are important in protecting the dune from erosion.*

3. *A sand dune is also prime habitat for the deer tick. Check yourself for the presence of ticks shortly after each visit.*

NOTES: _____

_____

_____

_____

_____

_____

_____

_____

_____

_____

The Effects of Waves

As the wind blows across the ocean surface it forms waves which change shape and size as they approach the coast. The bottom of the wave (trough) slows down as it reaches shallower waters. The top of the wave (crest) continues to move faster and then breaks along the shore. Here the impact of the waves will help determine the structure of the beach, forming either sandy, muddy, or rocky shores. This, in turn, will determine what animal species can live there.

1. Observe the waves at several sandy beaches.

2. Does it appear that the waves are moving in a straight line or at an angle?

3. When the waves hit the edge of the shoreline, do they remove any sediment? If you stand at the edge with bare feet, you can feel the movement of sand.

4. Is the sand moved to another part of the beach, taken off shore, or re-deposited at the same location?

5. Animals that live in this environment must be able to adapt to the shifting substrate. Dig in the sand and look for small mole crabs (*Emerita talpoida*), a small arthropod with an egg-shaped body and conspicuous antennae. Put any mole crabs that you collect in a bucket with a small amount of seawater.

6. Place a small mound of sand in the bucket. How do the mole crabs respond? Now release the animals back onto the beach. Observe their behavior.

7. Compare your observations here with those at a rocky shoreline.

8. Why is there very little sand present?

9. Look under some of the rocks for the presence of green crabs (*Carcinus maenus*) or Asian shore crabs (*Hemigrapsus sanguineus*).

10. Collect at least ten green crabs and measure the length of their shells (carapace). Calculate the average.

11. Are most of these young crabs or more mature?

12. How are they adapted to wave activity on this beach?

NOTES: _____

_____

_____

_____

_____

_____

_____

_____

What's in a Seine?

A beach seine is a long vertical net with wooden poles on each end, a set of weights on the bottom, and several floats on top. It is carried  NVS through the water by two people, one on each end. The seine is moved parallel to the shore and then brought up on the beach to see what animals have been trapped. The length of the seine and the mesh size varies.

1. Before using a seine, check out the area for small animals. Do you see schools of minnows or tiny crabs in the water?

2. Take the seine and walk out past these small animals.

3. Lining up parallel to the beach, move the seine slowly through the water.

4. Be sure that the bottom end of the pole is a few feet ahead of the top.

5. Also be extra careful that the weights and net drag along the bottom or many of the small fish will swim underneath and escape.

6. As you approach the shore, drag the net carefully over the sand and lift it once you reach the edge of the beach.

7. Move the net away from the water and check to see what you've caught.

8. Look for the following animals:
    a. mummichog fish
    b. silverside fish
    c. pipefish
    d. puffer fish
    e. shrimp
    f. small crabs
    g. comb jellies
    h. jellyfish   *(Do not touch jellyfish!)*

GDN

9. Some animals may be entangled in seaweed, so carefully look through the algae.

10. What was the most common animal caught?

11. What was the most unusual find?

12. Try a different section of the same beach. Do you see any differences in the animals collected?

13. Describe the substrate or bottom of the shoreline. Was it sandy, muddy, or rocky?

14. Do you find any differences when seining at different tides?

NOTES: _____

_____

_____

_____

_____

_____

_____

_____

What's up Dock?

Pilings on docks and piers provide interesting habitats for many marine plants and animals. The organisms exhibit a vertical zonation or distribution on the piling, particularly after several years of colonization. Some of the animals are confined to this habitat which is stationary and is characterized by a relatively constant physical environment. Over time the entire piling will be covered with an impressive assortment of marine species.

NVS

1. Locate a piling that is periodically exposed at low tide. Abandoned pilings are often inhabited by many species.

2. Do a quick survey of the piling. What algae and animal species do you see?

3. Which ones seem to be abundant?

4. Are any of the species confined to one section of the piling?

5. Are these closer to the water surface or are they located on the upper portions of the piling?

6. Look for the following animal species:
   a) Sea vase (*Ciona intestinalis*) - a nearly transparent vase-shaped filter feeder.

   b) Hydroids (*Tubularia spp.*) - small clumps or colonies of animals with pinkish polyps.

   c) Rock barnacles (*Semibalanus balanoides*) - filter-feeding crustaceans that capture food particles with tiny feathery feet.

7. Look for the following algae species:
   a) Sea lettuce (*Ulva lactuca*) - large green sheets that often fold along the edge.
   b) Irish moss (*Chondrus crispus*) - a deeply red to purple alga with many flat blades that can measure up to four inches long.

8. Are there any spider crabs (*Libinia emarginata*) present? This animal has a brown carapace (shell) and long, spindly legs.

9. If present do the spider crabs remain in one place or are they moving up and down the piling?

10. Can you tell what they are feeding on?

11. Are there any mollusks present such as blue mussels (*Mytilus edulis*) or oyster drills (*Urosalpinx cinereus*)?

12. Are there any bare patches along the length of the piling? What could cause this?

13. What physical factors affect the distribution of animals along the piling?

14. Compare your observations with another piling nearby. Do you see a different assemblage of living things or are they similar?

NOTES: _____

_____

_____

_____

_____

_____

The Plot Thickens

Different groups and communities of marine species can be identified and compared by selecting a study area along a marine system such as a sandy beach, sand dune, or salt marsh. Comparing one sample plot to another can show changes that have taken place, a phenomenon called succession. Usually these plots are measured in units of square meters but any size area can be studied.

NVS

1. Select an area that seems to have several species present.

2. Measure and mark off the area with string or ribbon.

3. Count the number of different plants and animals in the study plot.

4. Next count the number of individuals for each species.

5. If it's a common plant like beach grass, estimate what percent it covers the plot.

6. On a piece of paper draw a square and label one meter on each side.

7. Measure out a one meter square in the plot.

8. Create a set of symbols, a different one for each animal and plant.

NVS

9. On the paper write in the symbol for each species you see.

10. How are the species distributed in the plot? Would you describe them as uniform, random, or clumped?

11. Now count the number of individuals for each species. This tells you the density of the plant or animal per meter squared. (Density=the number of individuals divided by the area or D=N/A).

12. Do another plot and make the same calculations.

13. How do the two areas differ?

14. What environmental conditions allow some organisms to exist in the plot and not others? For example, does the substrate differ? Is wave action stronger in one section over another?

NOTES: _____

_____

_____

_____

_____

_____

_____

_____

_____

_____

_____

_____

_____

_____

ABOUT THE AUTHOR

Gilbert Newton, a Cape Cod native, has been teaching environmental and marine science at Sandwich High School and Cape Cod Community College for many years. His classes include coastal ecology, botany, coastal zone management, and environmental technology. In 2013 he became the first Director of the Sandwich STEM Academy. Gil has also taught classes for Massachusetts Maritime Academy, Falmouth Academy, Bridgewater State University, and Waquoit Bay National Estuarine Research Reserve. He was the Program Director for the Advanced Studies and Leadership Program at Massachusetts Maritime Academy for 14 years.

One of the founders of the Barnstable Land Trust, Gil is past president of the Association to Preserve Cape Cod. He completed his graduate work in biology at Florida State University. Gil is the author of several books about the Cape's shoreline including the recent *Mysteries of Seaweed*.

ABOUT THE PHOTOGRAPHER

Chris Dumas has lived and worked on Cape Cod for many years, teaching earth and space science at Sandwich High School. He is an advisor to the photography club there. Photography has been an important part of his life, traveling around the country in search of interesting vistas. Chris has a graduate degree in Resource Conservation from the University of Montana and is a native of the St. Lawrence River region of New York. His photography can be seen in several books including the recent *Mysteries of Seaweed*.

RECOMMENDED BOOKS

Barbo, Theresa Mitchell. *Cape Cod Wildlife*. The History Press. Charleston, South Carolina. 2012.

Gosner, Kenneth L. *A Field Guide to the Atlantic Seashore*. Houghton Mifflin Company. New York. 1978.

Newton, Gilbert. *Seaweeds of Cape Cod Shores: A Field Guide*. West Barnstable Press, Massachusetts. 2008.

Newton, Gilbert. *Marine Habitats of Cape Cod*. West Barnstable Press, Massachusetts. 2017.

Petry, Loren C. and Norman, Marcia G. *A Beachcomber's Botany*. The Chatham Press, Old Greenwich, Connecticut. 1963.

Schwarzman, Beth. *The Nature of Cape Cod*. University Press of New England. Lebanon, New Hampshire. 2002.

Tiner, Ralph W. Jr. *A Field Guide to Coastal Wetland Plants of the Northeastern United States*. The University of Massachusetts. Amherst, Massachusetts. 1987.

Zinn, Donald J. *Marine Mollusks of Cape Cod*. Cape Cod Museum of Natural History. Brewster, Massachusetts. 1984.

BOOKS BY GILBERT NEWTON

Seaweeds of
Cape Cod
Shores

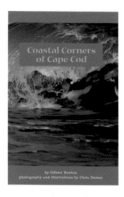

Coastal
Corners of
Cape Cod

The Ecology of
a Cape Cod
Salt Marsh

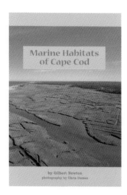

Marine
Habitats of
Cape Cod

Discovering
the Cape Cod
Shoreline

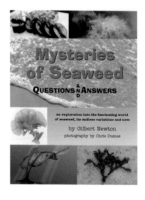

Mysteries of
Seaweed:
Questions and
Answers

All books are published by West Barnstable Press.

This book was designed and typeset by West Barnstable Press, www.westbarnstablepress.com. The font used for the title is a playful 1960s favorite, **Ad Lib**, which was designed by Freeman Craw for American Type Founders in 1994. The text font is **American Typewriter**, built by Joel Kaden and Tony Stan for International Typeface Corporation in 1974. It is a nod to manual typewriters. But, unlike the type of those vintage type-producing machines, the font has proportional sizing (all letters are not the same width). Photo credits were set in **Frutiger**, designed by Swiss typographer Adrian Frutiger (1928-2015). *Activities for the Cape Cod Beachcomber* was printed on 100 lb. white matte stock with a 12 pt. laminated cover.

Printed on recycled paper